MIGHTY ANIMAL MIGRATIONS

A HUMMINGBIRD'S JOURNEY

David and Julie Lavender

Enslow PUBLISHING

Please visit our website, www.enslow.com. For a free color catalog of all our high-quality books, call toll free 1-800-398-2504 or fax 1-877-980-4454

Published in 2027 by
Enslow Publishing
2544 Clinton Street
Buffalo, NY 14224

Cataloging-in-Publication Data
Names: Lavender, David R., 1961-, author. | Lavender, Julie, author.
Title: A hummingbird's journey / by David and Julie Lavender.
Description: Buffalo, NY : Enslow Publishing, 2027. | Series: Mighty animal migrations | Includes glossary.
Identifiers: ISBN 9781978549517 (pbk.) | ISBN 9781978549524 (library bound) | ISBN 9781978549531 (ebook)
Subjects: LCSH: Ruby-throated hummingbird--Migration--Juvenile literature.
Classification: LCC QL696.A558 L384 2027 | DDC 598.7641568--dc23

Photo credits: Cover, p 1 detchana wangkheeree (sky)/Shutterstock.com, Fiona M. Donnelly (Hummingbird)/Shutterstock.com; p 4 Monica Lara/Shutterstock.com, Meloday Mellinger/Shutterstock.com, MelandiWright/Shutterstock.com; p 5 Fiona M. Donnelly/Shutterstock.com; p 6 Travis Potter/Shutterstock.com; p 7 Stefan Schug/Shutterstock.com; p 8 RobDemPhoto/Shutterstock.com; p 9 Agnieszka Bacal/Shutterstock.com; p 10 Wirestock Creators/Shutterstock.com; p 11 Fiona M. Donnelly/Shutterstock.com; p 12 Krumpelman Photography/Shutterstock.com; p 13 Travis Potter/Shutterstock.com; p 14 Jennifer-Davis/Shutterstock.com; p 15 TMEwen/Shutterstock.com; p 16 VEAZ12/Shutterstock.com; p 17 Bonnie Taylor Barry/Shutterstock.com; p 18 Mike Truchon/Shutterstock.com; p 19 David Byron Keener/Shutterstock.com, sanjaya pushpakumara/Shutterstock.com; p 20 21 Daniel James Anderson/Shutterstock.com; p 22 Agnieszka Bacal/Shutterstock.com; p 23 FotoRequest/Shutterstock.com; p 24 Daniel R. Ripplinger/Shutterstock.com; p 25 Sari ONeal/Shutterstock.com; p 26 Danita Delimont/Shutterstock.com; p 27 jitkagold/Shutterstock.com; p 29 Radzas2008/Shutterstock.com, Aniko Gerendi Enderle/Shutterstock.com; p 30 Aniko Gerendi Enderle/Shutterstock.com

Printed in China

CPSIA compliance information: Batch #QSENS27: For further information, contact Enslow Publishing, New York, New York, at 1-800-398-2504.

Table of Contents

Winged Journey

Millions of animals move long distances every year. They search for food or better weather conditions. Some animals migrate across land. Other animals swim through the sea. And some, like the ruby-throated hummingbird, fly over both land and sea.

Herds of wildebeests and caribou migrate in groups. Geese and swans migrate together in flocks. But the tiny hummingbird migrates alone.

Ruby-throated hummingbirds leave North America in the fall. They take a dangerous journey over the Gulf of America. They stay in Mexico and Central America until they fly north again in the spring.

Costa's hummingbird

Anna's hummingbird

black-chinned hummingbird

ruby-throated hummingbird

Hummingbird Headlines

The ruby-throated hummingbird is just one type of hummingbird. More than 350 hummingbird **species** make their home in North America and South America. The birds get their name from the humming sound of their fast, flapping wings.

A Tiny Life Begins

On a cool May morning in Rhode Island, a tiny egg cracks. A small ruby-throated hummingbird pecks her way out. The hummingbird chick is less than one inch (2.54 cm) long and weighs very little. It would take three hummingbird chicks to weigh as much as one dime.

The mother hummingbird keeps her chick warm by staying in the nest most of the day. The new chick does not have feathers yet. Her eyes are closed. Her legs aren't strong enough to stand.

But one thing she can do? Beg for food!

Hummingbird Headlines

A tiny hummingbird chick still inside an egg has very strong neck muscles. It has a small, sharp hook on its short bill. When it is time to hatch, the chick pokes the eggshell over and over with the hook to make its way out of the egg.

A Whole New World

Hummingbird chicks need to eat about every 20 minutes. The mother hummingbird leaves the nest to drink nectar. She gobbles up gnats, small spiders, and mosquitoes for protein. She eats fruit flies, small bees, caterpillars, and aphids too.

The mother hummingbird returns to the nest. The new chick leans her head back and opens her mouth. The mother hummingbird pushes her beak into the chick's mouth. She **regurgitates** the bugs and nectar she just ate. Yum!

In nine days, the hummingbird chick's eyes are open. Some feathers are growing in. Because she eats so often, she grows quickly.

Hummingbird Headlines

By the time a ruby-throated hummingbird chick is three days old, it has doubled in size. By five days old, it doubles in size again. And by eight days, doubled again. That takes a lot of food from the mother hummingbird!

Leaving the Nest

After three weeks, the hummingbird chick's body is covered with feathers. She's ready to fly! She moves to the edge of the nest, flaps her wings, and leaves. The ruby-throated hummingbird is a **fledgling** now.

The hummingbird fledgling flies beside her mother. She watches her mother catch a mosquito in the air. The fledgling tries to catch a fly, but misses. She'll need more practice.

The chick follows the mother hummingbird to a patch of cardinal flowers. She pushes her beak into the flower, just like her mother. She laps up sweet nectar with her long, forked tongue.

On Her Own

With just one week of practice, the new hummingbird can flap her wings 50 times a second. She flies forward and backward. She can hover in front of bee balm or honeysuckle and drink nectar.

She **forages** for insects on her own now. The mother hummingbird has flown away to build a new nest.

The ruby-throated hummingbird spends the rest of summer flitting from flower to flower and catching bugs.

Hummingbird Headlines

Female ruby-throated hummingbirds lay one **clutch** of eggs at the beginning of summer. They usually have time to lay another before summer ends. When she lays eggs, she'll usually lay two at a time.

Shorter Days Cue Migration

As summer ends, the days become shorter. **Instinct** tells the hummingbird that migration time is near. She prepares for the long journey with extra nectar and more insects.

Now, it's time for the big migration! The ruby-throated hummingbird begins the journey south. She flies low, just above the treetops. When she spots a nectar-filled plant, she darts from blossom to blossom to drink. She stops often during the day for nectar. She rests at night.

Hummingbird Headlines

Ruby-throated hummingbirds can fly at speeds of 25 miles (40 km) per hour.

The Journey Across the Water

When the hummingbird makes it all the way to southern Georgia, she drinks extra nectar. She stores energy to make the trip across the Gulf of America.

For miles and miles, the hummingbird flies over water. Strong winds from a hurricane toss the tiny hummingbird off course. Rain soaks her small body. But she has to keep flying.

The hummingbird spots an oil rig and lands to rest. But she can't stay long. She pushes on, trying to get back on course. Hours later, she lands on a fishing boat for another short rest.

Hummingbird Headlines

The trip across the Gulf of America is about 500 miles (804 km). Hummingbirds must fly non-stop for about 20 hours to cross the water. Some ruby-throated hummingbirds take the long route along the coastline and only fly over land during the migration.

Winter Home

Soon, the hummingbird sees land ahead. She's made it to Mexico!

Weak. Tired. Hungry. The ruby-throated hummingbird finds a trumpet creeper vine and slurps nectar. She drinks and drinks.

The hummingbird spends the winter months in Mexico. It's warmer and flowers are plentiful. When spring arrives, it's time for her to migrate north. With lots of nectar and many insects, she stores up extra fat. She'll need the energy to make the long journey back across the Gulf of America.

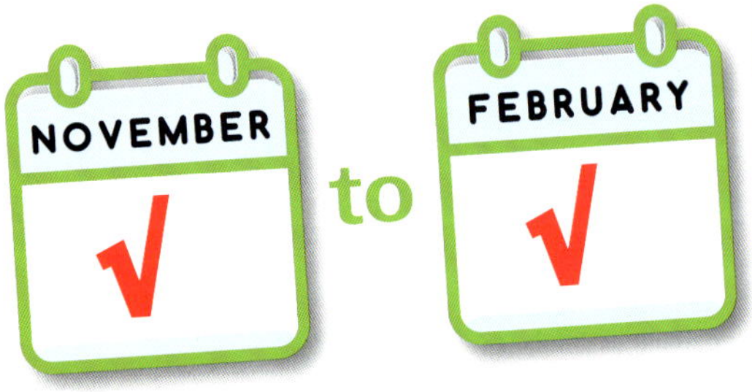

Flying North

Once again, the hummingbird takes flight across miles and miles of water. She flies without stopping for almost 20 hours. When she finally makes it to Florida, she drinks nectar from firebush plants and coral honeysuckle vines. Insects are plentiful too.

The ruby-throated hummingbird flies back to Rhode Island. She stops for nectar along the way and rests at night.

Once in Rhode Island, she mates. She builds a nest on a branch. She uses spider web silk, plant down, and moss.

Hummingbird Headlines

A hummingbird nest is cup-shaped and very small. It doesn't have to be very big because hummingbirds are the smallest birds in the world.

New Ruby-Throated Hummingbirds

The ruby-throated hummingbird lays two small eggs, no bigger than two jelly beans. She **incubates** the eggs to keep them warm. She only leaves the nest for five minutes every hour to forage for nectar and insects.

After 16 days, a tiny crack appears in one egg. Then, the same happens in the other. Two new hummingbirds hatch.

In one month, the new chicks can survive on their own. The ruby-throated hummingbird will fly off to mate again and lay another clutch of eggs.

Taking Flight Again

When the second brood of chicks leaves the nest, the ruby-throated hummingbird spends another week teaching her offspring how to find nectar and catch insects. Then, she flies away, leaving them on their own.

She'll drink nectar and search for caterpillars, spiders, and insects. She needs to store up extra fat for the next migration.

With one cycle complete, the migration journey begins again. It's time to fly south for the winter.

Hummingbird Headlines

Hummingbirds have other dangers besides a difficult migration. Sometimes, they crash into buildings while flying. Or they may be eaten by hawks, praying mantises, orb weaver spiders, cats, and other **predators**.

Over Land and Over Sea

Adult ruby-throated hummingbirds weigh about as much as a penny. Their **wingspan** is only three to four inches (7.6 to 10.1 cm). They may be small birds, but they are mighty fliers.

They dart from flower to flower with wings flapping about 50 times per second. They fly forward and backward. They can hover in one place and stop quickly when necessary.

But perhaps their most amazing feat is flying non-stop for 20 hours across the Gulf of America. Their migration takes them over land and sea. And they do it well.

A Hummingbird Migration Map

1. Ruby-throated hummingbirds are born in late spring and summer in southern Canada and in the eastern half of the United States.
2. In the fall, ruby-throated hummingbirds begin a long journey south in preparation for the winter months.
3. The hummingbirds fly over land until they reach the Gulf of America.
4. Some hummingbirds take a longer route and stay over land to reach Mexico.
5. But most make the long journey across the Gulf of America by flying non-stop for 18 to 22 hours.
6. Ruby-throated hummingbirds spend the winter in parts of Mexico and Central America.
7. In the spring, ruby-throated hummingbirds begin their journey north again to mate, lay eggs, and raise baby chicks in southern Canada and the eastern half of the United States.

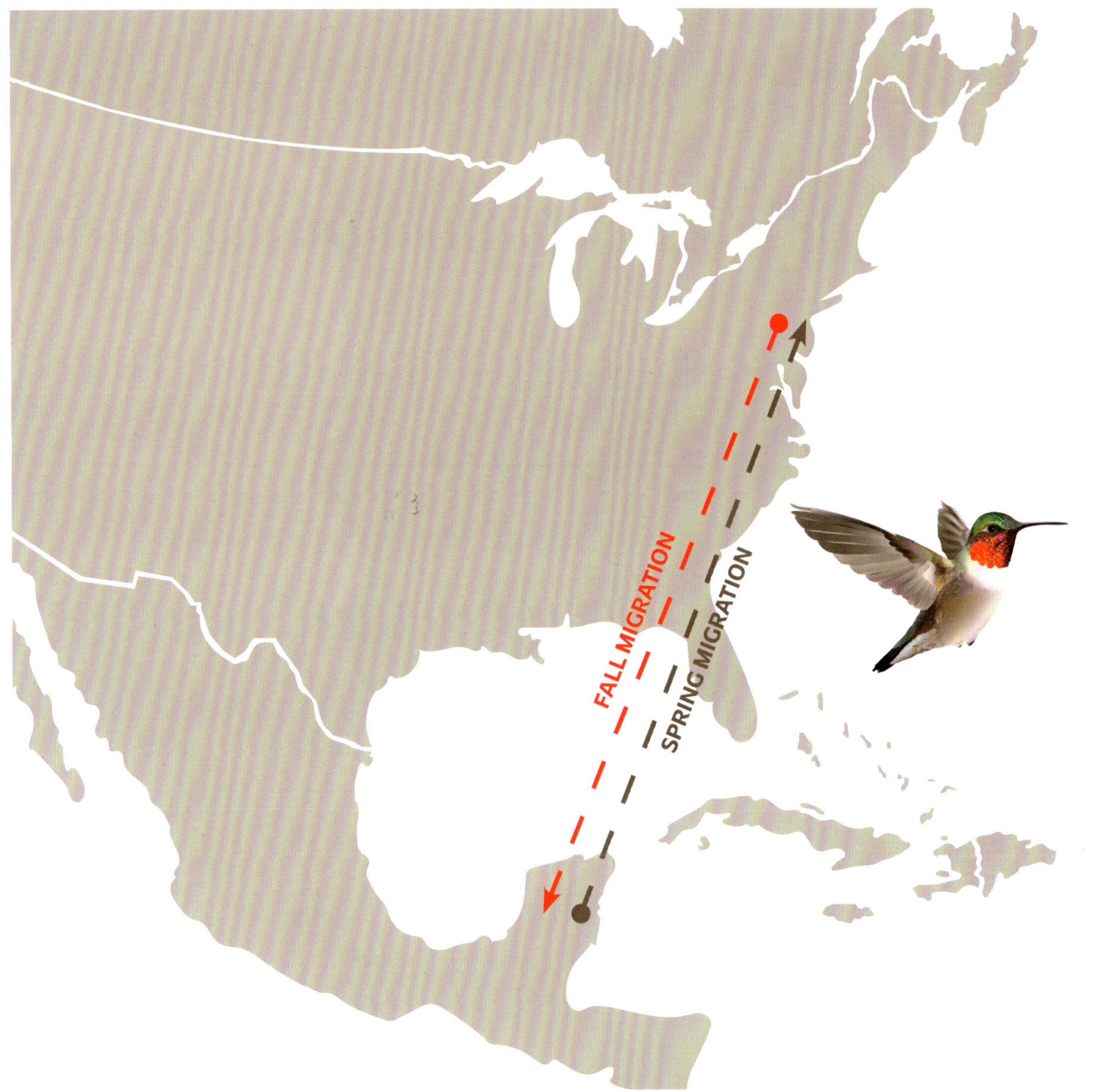
FALL MIGRATION
SPRING MIGRATION

Glossary

clutch (kluhch): a group of eggs laid in one nest by one female at the same time

fledgling (FLEH-jling): a young bird just learning to fly and ready to leave the nest

forages (FOR-uh-jiz): wanders around searching for food

incubates (ING-kyuh-bates): sits on eggs to keep them warm until time for them to hatch

instinct (IN-stingkt): behavior that is natural and not learned

predators (PRED-uh-turz): animals that live by hunting other animals for food

regurgitates (ri-GUR-juh-tates): to vomit up partially digested food

species (SPEE-sheez): a group of living things that are alike and can produce young together

wingspan (WING-span): the distance between the outer tips of a pair of wings of a bird, bat, or butterfly

Fact Check

1. Hummingbirds feed on insects and _________.
   a. seeds   b. nectar   c. nuts

2. When a young hummingbird is able to fly out of the nest, it's called a _______.
   a. fledgling   b. falcon   c. cub

3. An adult hummingbird can flap its __________ about 50 times per second.
   a. feet   b. tail   c. wings

Answers: 1. b, 2. a, 3. c

Further Reading

Baxter, Roberta. *Native Pollinators: Hummingbirds*. Mitchell Lane Publishers, 2020.

MacCarald, Clara. *Migrating to Survive*. ABDO Publishing, 2023.

Riggs, Kate. *Hummingbirds*. The Creative Company, 2022

On the Internet

Fun Facts about Hummingbirds

https://southwest.audubon.org/conservation/fun-facts-about-hummingbirds

Learn cool facts about hummingbirds.

Hummingbirds

https://nationalzoo.si.edu/migratory-birds/hummingbirds

Read tips about flowers that attract hummingbirds to a yard.

Index

About the Authors

David and Julie Lavender love watching ruby-throated hummingbirds zip, dive, and dart from flower to flower to backyard feeders. They've enjoyed placing hummingbird feeders in their yards in Georgia, Florida, North Carolina, and Virginia, and enjoyed spotting other hummingbird species when they lived in California and Washington State. The authors love all kinds of birds, but ruby-throated hummingbirds are one of their favorites. David and Julie enjoy writing about animals, visiting their kids and grandkids, and hiking new places. David's careers included working with animals as an entomologist and wildlife biologist, and Julie loved educating kids as a teacher and homeschooling mom.